Special Delivery

Elizabeth Kirkpatrick Vrenios

Gloria —
My gratitude for your
generous spirit, enthusiasm and
support in helping me get this
project off the ground —
Thank you !

Lizbeth

PUBLISHED BY YELLOW CHAIR PRESS

www.yellowchairreview.com

ISBN-13: 978-1532959073

ISBN-10: 1532959079

Printed in the United States of America

5606 Fairview Drive
Waco, Texas 76710

Cover Photo: The cover photo is a self-photo by Nicholas Vrenios, found 300 miles away from the Pan Am 103 crash by a North Umbrian hunter who caught it as it floated down from the sky. The photo was returned to Lockerbie, miraculously unscathed by the fire, smoke or rain that was present that evening.

Cover Design: Sarah Frances Moran

For all those who loved Nick

CONTENTS

ACKNOWLEDGMENTS

[I am grateful to the editors of the following journals in which these poems first appeared, sometimes in earlier versions:]

Clementine Poetry Journal, "Scarfskin"
Edison Literary Review, "Harvest," to be published Fall 2017
Kentucky Review "A Ledger Balanced"
Bethlehem Writers Roundtable, "Diminuendo and Crescendo in Blue"
The Binnacle, "Darling Icarus"
Evening Street Press, "Departure"

The poems in this chapbook are written about the events surrounding the bombing of Pan Am 103 over Lockerbie, Scotland, on Dec 21, 1988. Elizabeth's son Nicholas, a student at Syracuse University at the time, was returning home for the Christmas holidays after spending a semester abroad in England, and he was on that fatal flight. The final poem by Nicholas was written in 1988, the year he perished in the Lockerbie crash.

Departure

Through the peephole of stars
I see myself as I was,
clutching my gray woolen sweater about my throat
in my buttoned-up kitchen,
feeling the scant warmth of the winter sun,
stamping December's cold away.
I held tight to the phone's umbilical cord
connecting me to his voice, even then
sweet as the meat of an apple,
rich with victory whoops
as he dare-deviled down the street on his skateboard,
or bellowed his lusty songs from the bedroom
long after I called out to turn off the light.

My husband and I packed the car
and were eager to leave
to meet him at the airport.
I could barely restrain my impatience
at the irritant of the phone's ring
pulling me reluctantly
to answer
—and it was Nick,
his voice crackling from over the ocean.
A wave of restlessness washed over me
to push away the hours
before we could embrace
yet I didn't want the call to end
as I heard the faint toot of the horn.

Forgive me, Beloved, for what I could not see that day.
I could not see how close we were to the water's edge,
nor how soon the ocean would howl and churn.

I could not see how that cold December moon,
round as the apple of your voice,
would be sliced apart,
and how you would gallop away into the wind

and disappear,
to lie broken on Lockerbie's ground.

Darling Icarus

Riding his own dare
he exults on the brink

cradles the quarry
high on the stamen of the sun

whose brute music
stains him radiant

he ascends with burning wings
plumage spread circling

follows the winged sluice
like heaven's glass rims ringing

until midair tastes him
the boy at the whorl of the rose

plunges to the center of his universe
water jumps at his entrance

blue petal upon blue petal curving
at the bloom of the inner cliffs

he folds himself into innocence
the first to catch the stinging waters

Electric Song

Joy is an unexpected flowering,
    dogwood in the garden,
    a guest,
as I fold my morning,
    coffee dog-eared,
my book cold.

Like a multicolored bird,
joy returns to land in the pages at my feet
    exhilarated by flight,
its song, red as star-stone
warms me,
    a plum blossom windblown.

*

Joy comes to the lone pilot
    landing his craft on home soil,
the rattle-and-bang arrival
of a Nissan,
in battered mustard-yellow.

    Joy is the rousing yell
of the up-the-stair
    race,
to throw off cornered shadows
bounding me in sleep
taken to escape the burial of despair.

Like a child with a blue adventure ball,
joy, the lone chime,

releases its fragrant lilacs to the wind,
     water discovering fountain,
       purple nectar discovering
the yellow yellow bee.

The book of electric song is about to open,
     and the son,
his afternoon radiant in the wind
warms
this solitary stone.

Waiting to Hear

Where is the plane?
The agents will not tell you.
You try to hold it together,
gripping the Naugahyde arm,
your breath locked down,
willing your heavy heart to stop.

Their fumbling words
offer up fallacies for truth
behind the reality
of the exploding plane in midair.
No one story is the same
and you sit,
trying to hold the words together
while your drowning heart
keeps trying to swim to shore.

Later that evening, CNN broadcasts
everything you want to know
and more that you could not imagine
sharp in black and gray,
a plane in pieces,
fire everywhere,
and you sit
trying to hold your mind together,

and you are no longer swimming
but sink and sink and cannot hit bottom.

No glimpse of his body
in the thousand pictures
they constantly broadcast

only the same fluorescent words
trying to tell a story they cannot tell.
You attempt a courage
that doesn't give itself a name
and you sit,
and you wait,
trying to hold it together,
trying to hold him together:
his hands
his feet
his brown, brown eyes.

Terminal

rush toward the terminal's
long ticket counter
Where is the gate?
tight huddle of blue backs
stiffen
tallest sucks air through his teeth
and eyes closely,
demands
Why do you want to know?
My son is on the plane, his gate isn't posted.
blinding lights hover
above a sea of photographers
at the far wall
lights
blinding, dashing -
Look there's one! Get 'er picture!

*

last spark
cigarette crushed under his heel
Don't talk, Ma'am, just keep moving.
large fingers fold over wrist
pull through double doors
growls into walkie-talkie
I need more security STAT!
We have a relative here,
take her up to the waiting area.
his foot wedges
into open elevator door
three men crowd in

*

What has happened?
quick glance from eye to eye
one wipes his upper lip
We aren't authorized to tell you, Ma'am.
hands behind them
rigid as soldiers
eyes nailed to the ceiling
Has the plane been hijacked?
silence opens to a black hole
No, ma'am, just come with us.

*

door opens
large lounge, crowded
in huddled groups of two and three
escorted to a lone
leather couch,
Wait right here, Ma'am,
someone will join you shortly.
eyes tumble over doorknobs
empty coffee cups
faint murmurs
whisperings
soft wails

*

watch face rubbed
over and over
light shifting through
large windows
gives over to uncertain shadow
agent finally arrives

What has happened to the plane?

*

he sits on the edge
of the chair
rubs knuckles
Well, ma'am   there has been,
there has been...

---

an accident...
What kind of accident?

he swallows
An explosion

Small or large?
Large

Was the plane on the ground or in the air?
It was ...

---

in the air

soundless thunder begins
its descent

a voice...mine?
any survivors?

unraveled

nylons torn,   birkenstocks   red sweater tossed
aside
one mother knuckles
to her knees wailing
no one touches her

remembering this space   my body   with other people
afternoon sun forks   hearts stare   mute stones
weight of sorrow rings in our ears
settles on our thirsty
eyes   shoulders
dusting the tops of our shoes

i can't think   i must   i can't   can't think

her keening splatters the impassive
walls of the waiting room
swallowing each violet abyss
we become our own sorrow

i'm not here   a dream   i'm not here

the sky turns on its huge axis
scarlet lockerbie
our loss is blindness
counting broken and tumbled days

i know numbness   i know silence   i know nothing

women   always women
bear the burden
kneeling   screaming   fetal

embrace the space of   dead children
        grief passes through
their softness into air
i bend   i hesitate   i break

a litany of retaliations
movie star president   lame duck
nouveau john wayne
attack aircraft
air raid of libya
terrorists with suitcase eyes
ecstatic with visions
of detonators   bombs
rigid   unbending   ruthless
stoic radicals shackle life
together with smoke and barbed wire
impenetrable   eyes   heart
serpentine secret deep in the bowels of the plane

the world   garroted   unraveled
weeping   weeping   weeping
not for lost children
mothers brothers sons
but for innocence lost
no longer can
the vulnerable motherland
wraps its dusky arms
around rootless bodies

The Long Ride Home

The swollen moon peers
in the car windows, guiding our way home

on this cold December drive.

Dusk long ago pulled in its shadows
and we have miles more to go,

traveling to the edge of our own universe,
not knowing what lays beyond it.

Only the confounded moon, a lump
in the sky's throat,

seems to guide us.
The car swallows the miles behind us
and in front of us,

through two sharp, clean-edged
tunnels of light,

unbelieving, bewildered,
our hearts are broken, over and over.

We know this road,
this time,
will not cease to end.

I Hope It Rains

A slant of sun smears through the blinds.
It must be morning.

How slow it is, how heavy,
setting fire to motes
as I watch it inch
across the rumpled bed

slicing shadowed patterns
like a keen-edged stare.
I am still reluctant
to rouse.

Instead, I stare unmoved—
watch it crawl
across the quilt,
cross-stitching each square
into faded reds and blues,

brazen up the metallic table leg,
across the wallpaper's empty   yellow   roses
before descending
to gild the clouded glass,
still shrouded with the dirt-red dregs
of last night's wine.

At last it envelops
my blue-veined and spotted hands,
the hairs dancing a slow rise.

Special Delivery

Piles of detritus greet us at the "store":
Crumbling suitcases,
size 10 shoes,
skateboards without wheels,
all disfigured by smoke and fire
into gray clones of recollection.

Whispering, gray-footed Scots like shepherds
looking after their lost flocks,
tend mountains of clothing,
scrubbed and ironed for display
by caretakers who had labeled each:

Passenger "78" or "270" or "unknown."
We, half mad, stumble but still desperate
for the joy of finding one more spark of memory,
seek reminders of Nick.
No article fully recognizable,
given the measure of ash.

I point to a small green bottle labeled "R."
Are you sure it is yours?
I packed it as a surprise – he loved Paco Rabanne.

We see the time-line of recovery,
amended daily
by the devoted scavengers,
labeled and numbered
across the walls
in hand-drawn letters:
"passengers 1 through 270."
The bloody trail splayed

on the walls high above our heads.

How are they numbered? I ask.
By the ability to recognize them.
Where is our son?
Near 200.

The officers, sharp-eyed sheepdogs,
stare at us as we prepare to sort through
pictures taken by our son whose sphere
embraced us all.
There is a collective sharp intake of breath

as we see a large self-portrait of Nick
nestled on a pile of images, intact.
No ash or water has ravaged it.
No explosion has charred its surface.

It exists as if released when Nick ascended,
to float far above the chaos,
traveled for miles,
three hundred, perhaps,

until a Northumbrian hunter,
drenched by the Scottish storm, looked up
and stretched out his arms toward
the descending dispatch, catching it.

Oh, how Nick would have taken pleasure
in being set aloft as a scrap of paper,
his life now telescoped into an image:

he, sun-blessed, perched
on a rocky ledge above

the clouds, greeting us with
a Dewar's gin bottle in his hand,
and a grin as wide as heartbreak.

Diminuendo and Crescendo in Blue

The jazz of the chainsaw wounds
as the lop-limbed pines fold and tumble,
their silvery needles pushing down against the air,

bowing in genuflection.
The light from the newly uncovered sun
shyly illuminates my drive.

Each year there are fewer pines,
felled by rot, disease, or age

but I feel their loss
much like the forever green
of a child's back shored up

against mine,
the indent no longer
sculptured on his pillow.

I will get used to this blinding glare
slashing an unfamiliar swath
across my drive.

I might even bless it,
but those tall shadows—
how I will miss them!

A Ledger Balanced

We pass you from hand to hand,
brush the image of your smile caught
forever in these dog-eared snapshots.

How luminous you are here
in the odd flush of a mid-winter afternoon.
For a moment we breathe you

back into our lives as we read
your writing, indelible
in black-and-white composition books

you've stashed under the bed.
We were not certain we could bear to open them.
Cross-legged on the patchwork quilt

we turn each ink-stained page,
the words you wrote
burn like numinous comets

through our hearts,
leaving us blistered and hollow.
We can only keep the memory

of what has faded into final air,
your gesture here, waving us away.

The color of buttons and dark violet,
presses heavy as the woolen coat
we hold and send our fingers through,

just to feel the space of your body,

where it once was flesh and warmth.
As we name each moment yours,

a silent promise passes between us
to un-mention you:
a ledger balanced and put away,

a solace of hymns jailed in our throats.

I Only Need a Thimbleful More of Time

Each night I set the bedside clock back
set the clock back 2/1000ths of a second
2/1000ths of a second added each day
each day becoming longer than 24 hours
24 hours and 2/1000ths of a second today

Today will always be shorter than tomorrow
and tomorrow when I add on
and as I add on yet another one
yet another one strung out endlessly
endlessly like a mirrored hallway
a mirrored hallway reflecting itself
reflecting itself endlessly
endlessly I ask myself how

how can I gather them all
all the sub-eyeblink slowdowns together
together in a slender vein of moments to squander
squander in a tear-drop of day
the briefest day in which we embrace once more
so once more I can caress my son
my son with the forever eyes pool-deep and stunned
stunned eyes that didn't see the plane crash.

The crash that slowed the earth's spin
the spin slowed by 2/1000ths of a second
2/1000ths of a second each day for eons…
for eons… all the milliseconds
all the milliseconds of all the centuries
all the centuries of time in a thimble
a thimble of time weighing
weighing heavily

heavily upon me
upon me as I close my eyes
close my eyes.

Leatherbacks

A requiem silence burgeons
like mushrooms under our floorboards.
You and I keep hoping

this moment is only a rehearsal
but know it is not,
and always, always the somber river

of the never-ending present,
drowns us
in a long and silent streak,

leaving behind mute spaces
we tunnel into.
How is it we have
to pull ourselves into ourselves
and back

into our full-bodied shells
where our muted thoughts
un-finish our words?

We load the burden of the present
on our backs,
unable to drag ourselves

into tomorrow.

He Takes His Final Leave

Last night in my dreams,
I entered a yellow cave gilded
by the sun's bright window,
    and I saw him,
long absent from my sleep,
perched in a pine tree
growing inside the cave.

Its needled branches
cast sharp shadows
that punctured and pulled
    black threads through
the open weave of my heart.

(black-winged dream)

I looked up and saw
my will-o'-the-wisp
son, yoda-bodied,
    wizened and precarious,
high in the uppermost branches
that scraped the rocky ceiling.

(Black wings soared)

I heard his laughter,
    and sounds like bells
like yellow guitars
like the roar of an old jalopy,
    rained down

on my upturned face,

fracturing the air,
sending a chill through me
as if the sun had been darkened.

   (Black wings sting my cheeks)

Nick leapt from the flinty sky
with the grace of a fearless child
plummeting soft as a fire's plume.
Tumbling,
his golden hair in ashes,
      winked,
and with a tip of his soft mushroom hat,

   (weightless memory)

rollicked into the woods
around the corner at the edge
where the sun now rises over and over.

Time Squared

I am a runner
but the days gallop past me on horseback,
hide under beds and in tea cups,
burn with a red blooming light,

each square an unnamed cadaver
fluttering a toe tag of raggy deeds:

Monday: tomato soup
Tuesday: framed your picture
Wednesday: lunch and a movie.

Yesterday only slashed marks
chalked in my memory's fleeting deaths.
Without you each square is a darkened womb,

a dead man's loan,
but you disappear through holes
grown larger with years,

years squared by days, each abandoned.
How can it be
that you still come no closer

than I can bear?

Scarfskin

the outermost layer of the snakeskin
- Webster's New World Dictionary

I hold the opaque skin to the light,
striated, papery, colorless,
an ephemeral wing of a ghost.

The creature who inhabited you,
an undulating river of muscle
grown beyond the skin you knew,
now curving into the crust of the earth.

Brittle remnant of memory
like the husk shucked off the walnut
the rind peeled from the fruit.

How easily you cast it off and disappear,
kissing the earth with your soft mouth.

All that is left of you is
the fragile skin I hold in my hands,
leaving my longing: a deeper hunger
than your instinct to shed.

Back at the Music School Office after Christmas Vacation

I climb from the car,
stretch my legs like a wintered spider,
and blink to accustom myself
to the new slant of light.
The leaves in the parking lot rush to greet me,
brush against the tops of my shoes
and swirl around my ankles.

As I push through the heavy glass doors,
I see the secretary's desk
empty-
too early for her arrival.
No sound
save the driving arpeggios
of a lone pianist in the distance.

Only a month gone. Who am I?
Who is this grey mouse
who drags her wet wooly heart behind her,
and now tiptoes down the long hallway
as if walking were a sacrilege
and breathing a sin?
When did the block walls fade to grey?
When did the rooms grow so far apart?

The last month has curled up and tumbled away,
yellow giving way to brown,
to black,
leaving me startled at the jumble of unopened letters,
the piles of red-pocked term papers
stacked on my desk,

the tethered phone
blinking incessantly.

I remove the sign on my door:
DO NOT ENTER: MUSICIAN WORKING
and scrape off the sticky remnants
of tape that still outline the now empty square.
I take down the helter-skelter posters,
and the out-of-date notices
that jostle each other for attention,
leaving the nude cork raw,
stubbled with thumbtacks.

The clock snaps to attention at 9:00.
The students begin to arrive
in streams of loopy yellow,
barging through the front doors,
red knots of giggles
and unintended rudeness.
I feel ragged and soft,
unfamiliar in this familiar world,
still trying to shake off images of a burning plane,
and a fog-shrouded bagpiper climbing the hill
next to an empty hole in the ground.

How strange it is to be here,
for I have returned like a prodigal daughter
from a distant shore,
having been garroted by the cruelty of the world.

The first student of the semester
knocks sharply on the door and as she enters
lowering her self-conscious eyes,
I swallow deep into my bones.

I straighten my skirt,
look up
and smile.

Harvest

*The heart, like the grape, is prone to delivering its harvest in the same
moment that it appears to be crushed.*—Roger Housden

Dearest , I love the harvest
beyond the harvest
more than the heart can bear,
yet do not wish to relinquish you
to the one who reaps.

You and I, Beloved,
were created joyously,
from sand and ash and forged by fire
to become transparent chalices
containing this full-bodied claret wine.

We have been sleepwalking, my darling,
as if death were not on our shoulders.
Our ringing glasses, where we once drank deeply
are now drained, shattered.

What else is there to do
but throw up our arms and sing
as we climb through the jubilant sky
toward morning?

Such Splendor

Such a brilliant ball of fire.
It glowed with rainbow colors
as it plumaged to the earth
in the dim blue sky.
It appeared significantly inspiring
as if to give my life meaning.
Wondrous and mysterious, for I
have never witnessed such a splendor.

Nicholas Andreas Vrenios
August 20, 1968 – December 21, 1988

41

ABOUT THE AUTHOR

Elizabeth Kirkpatrick Vrenios' poetry has appeared in such on line and print journals as *Clementine*, *Silver Birch Press*, *Kentucky Review*, *Bethlehem Writers Roundtable*, *Poeming Pidgeon* and *Silkworm*, and in forthcoming issues of *Edison Literary Review*, and *Unsplendid*. She was recently featured in Tupelo Press's 30/30 challenge, and has co-written the book *Party Line* under the name Elizabeth Kirkpatrick. Elizabeth is a Professor Emerita from The American University in Washington DC, having chaired the vocal and music departments. Kirkpatrick Vrenios' solo recitals throughout the United States, South America, Scandinavia, Japan and Europe have been acclaimed, and as the artistic director of the Redwoods Opera Workshop in Mendocino, California, and the Crittenden Opera Workshop in Washington D.C. and Boston, she has influenced and trained students across the country. She is a member of the international Who's Who of Musicians, and is the past National President of the National Opera Association. She resides in Bethesda, Maryland with her son Christopher and grandson, Nicholas.

31953568R00025

Made in the USA
Middletown, DE
17 May 2016